HURRICANE

RAF Fighter

Photographs by Dan Patterson
Text by Air Vice-Marshal Ron Dick

The BOSTON
MILLS PRESS

Copyright © Ron Dick, 2000
Photographs copyright © Dan Patterson, 2000

Cataloging in Publication Data

Dick, Ron, 1931-
   Hurricane : RAF Fighter

Includes bibliographical references.
ISBN 1-55046-356-X

1. Hurricane (Fighter planes). 2. World War, 1939-1945 – Aerial operations, British.
I. Patterson, Dan, 1953-   . II. Title

UG1242.F5D53 2000   358.4'383   00-931861-5

04 03 02 01 00   1   2   3   4   5

Published in 2000 by
Boston Mills Press
132 Main Street
Erin, Ontario
N0B 1T0
Tel 519-833-2407
Fax 519-833-2195
e-mail books@bostonmillspress.com
www.bostonmillspress.com

An affiliate of
Stoddart Publishing Co. Limited
34 Lesmill Road
Toronto, Ontario, Canada
M3B 2T6
Tel 416-445-3333
Fax 416-445-5967
e-mail gdsinc@genpub.com

Distributed in Canada by
General Distribution Services Limited
325 Humber College Boulevard
Toronto, Ontario
M9W 7C3
Orders 1-800-387-0141 Ontario & Quebec
Orders 1-800-387-0172 NW Ontario
                 & other provinces
e-mail cservice@genpub.com

Distributed in the United States by
General Distribution Services Inc.
PMB 128, 4500 Witmer Industrial Estates
Niagara Falls, New York 14305-1386
Toll-free 1-800-805-1083
Toll-free fax 1-800-481-6207
e-mail gdsinc@genpub.com
www.genpub.com

Design by Dan Patterson

Printed in Hong Kong

THE CANADA COUNCIL | LE CONSEIL DES ARTS
FOR THE ARTS | DU CANADA
SINCE 1957 | DEPUIS 1957

We acknowledge for their financial support of
our publishing program the Canada Council,
the Ontario Arts Council, and the Government of
Canada through the Book Publishing Industry
Development Program (BPIDP).

CONTENTS

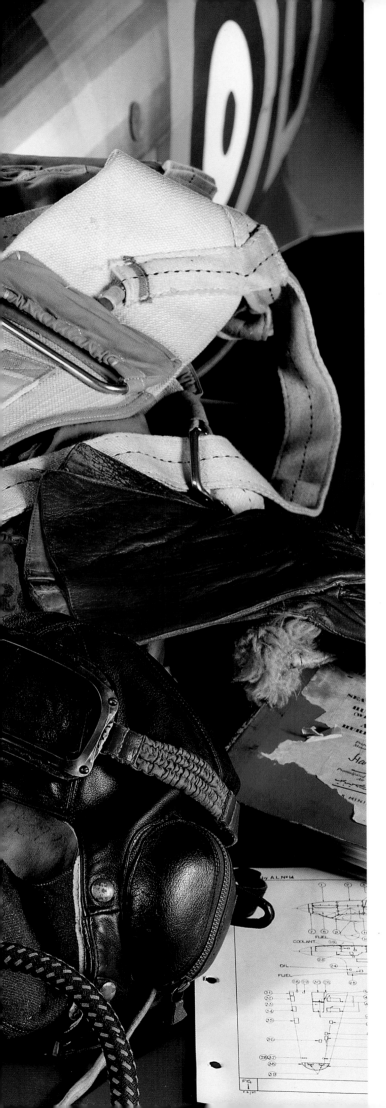

PREFACE

This is the first in a new series of Boston Mills Press aviation books. The Flying History books invite readers to view famous aircraft such as the Hawker Hurricane through the window provided to us by the owners and restoration craftsmen and women who keep these rare examples of flying history in the air. Modern lenses and films offer a much crisper image and allow us to see the hardware with a fresh vision and the perspective of history.

More important than the use of new technology and restored airplanes are the "living historians." We who have the advantage of looking back on events past should not forget that these famous aircraft are the creations of people who had a problem to solve. The results of their efforts were the fighters, bombers and transports that have become legendary and now reside in a place of honor in museums and memory. These airplanes, which became weapons of war, were the tools given to very young men to complete the tasks and duties assigned to them. Each of these airplanes made it off the ground only because of the work of many individuals, men and women trained in service to their countries, to keep the engines running, the guns armed and re-armed, to repair the damage of battle and, finally, to fly and fight.

I have followed the restoration of the Hurricane for several years. The opportunity to watch the Hurricane come back to life and also to allow readers to see inside this famous fighter has been a truly unique experience. In May of this year, when the beautifully finished airplane was rolled out into the daylight and onto the grass, there was a collective moment of wonder for all who were there. You can imagine what it was like, to see this creation of another time come alive once more.

Craig Charleston climbs into the cockpit, goes through the checklist, and soon from the Hurricane comes the whine of pumps and clatter of valves and connectors, the sound of a Rolls-Royce Merlin engine about to start. Slowly the prop begins to turn, the three blades now whirling into a gray disk. The engine catches and blue smoke erupts from the exhaust stacks. Close your eyes, and the roar of the Merlin transforms a quiet Suffolk hilltop into a forward fighter landing ground during the summer of 1940.

Dan Patterson, 1 July 2000

Artifacts and a pilot's personal flying kit displayed on the tailplane of a Hurricane. From the left, an Irvin sheepskin-lined flying jacket. Resting on top of the jacket, two essential pieces of survival gear, the "Mae West" life vest and parachute harness. The broad band over the left shoulder holds the D-ring that the pilot would pull to release the chute. At right-center, the leather gauntlets. Below are the pilot's flying helmet and goggles; attached to the helmet, the oxygen mask made from chamois and fabric.

HAWKER HURRICANE

In June 1936 the name Hurricane was formally adopted for the Hawker Aircraft Company's new monoplane fighter. It was an appropriate choice for an aircraft that was to find itself repeatedly in the eye of the most intense storms of World War II. Hurricanes were in the front line from the first day of the war to the last, fighting in every theater and in many different roles. Much loved by their pilots, they were rugged, adaptable and maneuverable, and among the steadiest aerial gun platforms ever designed. Yet despite their admirable qualities and the extent of their contribution to the eventual Allied victory, they have not always received the recognition they deserve. Perhaps not as photogenic as Supermarine's Spitfire, nor as menacing as the Messerschmitt Bf109, and not as fast as either, the Hurricane has been too often characterized as a "workhorse," a term that hints at its capacity to carry the weight of a battle but says little of its effectiveness in attack. The historical record tells a different story. The Hurricane would be better called a warhorse, an aerial Bucephalus upon whose efforts one of the most crucial victories in the history of human conflict was built. Without Hawker's resilient monoplane fighter, the Battle of Britain could not have been won, and the world would almost certainly have become a very different place.

A FAMILY ESTABLISHED

The Hurricane's lineage can be traced through a series of distinguished fighter aircraft to the years before World War I. It was in 1912 that Thomas Sopwith founded the Sopwith Aviation Company. The organization's first home was in a building that had been a skating rink at Kingston-upon-Thames, near London. Tom Sopwith had already made a name for himself as one of Britain's leading pioneer aviators, and he believed he could turn his celebrity to good account in building and selling his own aeroplanes. At an early stage in the life of his company, he hired a young Australian pilot named Harry Hawker. The choice was a good one, and Hawker proved to be an invaluable asset. During WWI, Hawker was responsible for testing every type of aircraft produced by the Sopwith company.

The first of Sopwith's designs to catch the public eye was the Tabloid, a neat little biplane that made its debut at Hendon in 1913. One year later, fitted with floats, it attracted international headlines by winning the Schneider Trophy in Monaco, easily outperforming its much-fancied Deperdussin and Nieuport monoplane rivals. A number of Tabloids saw service with both the Royal Flying Corps and the Royal Naval Air Service, but, remarkable though they were for the time, their limitations as military aircraft were soon made apparent by wartime developments. Sopwith accordingly turned his attention to producing an effective combat aircraft. The result was a nimble single-seater called the Pup, which arrived on squadrons in 1916 and played its part in ending the period of German air superiority known as the Fokker Scourge. The Pup was the immediate ancestor of the most famous of Sopwith's little biplanes, the Camel, which was credited with more aerial victories than any other fighter of either side during WWI. By 1918 the Camel had been followed by the Dolphin, an armored ground-attack aircraft, and the Snipe, a formidable fighter in the agile tradition of the Camel that remained in service for several years after the war ended.

The postwar period saw a massive reduction in defense spending and therefore in orders for new military aircraft. The Sopwith company was one of those especially hard hit and forced into liquidation. Undeterred, Tom Sopwith began again, forming a new company, under the name H. G. Hawker Engineering in recognition of the valuable work done by his chief test pilot. Sadly, Hawker did not live to see the venture succeed. He was killed while practising for a Hendon air show in July 1921. The company that bore his name, however, survived the difficulties of the early 1920s to build a solid reputation for producing dependable aircraft.

Sydney Camm, designer of the Hurricane.

CAMM CHARTS THE COMPANY'S COURSE

By 1923 the chief designer at Hawker's was George Carter, who in November of that year hired a young man named Sydney Camm to be a senior draftsman. Having spent nine years employed by the Martinsyde company, where he began as an apprentice in 1914, Camm now set out on what was to be his life's work. In a relationship with Hawker's that lasted forty-three years, he worked on the designs of a wide range of aircraft from the two-seat Cygnet biplane to the Harrier VTOL fighter – a record of achievement which included fifty-two types and some 26,000 individual aircraft.

Camm replaced Carter as Hawker's chief designer in 1925 and began to concentrate his efforts on military designs. The classic Hawker biplanes sprang from his fertile mind – Heron, Hornbill, Hawfinch, Hart and, the most aesthetically pleasing of the biplane fighters, the Fury. In 1933, after the company name had been shortened to Hawker Aircraft Limited, Camm began considering the advantages to be gained from moving on to a monoplane design. Discussions with the Air Ministry failed to garner official support for the proposal, but Hawker's board grasped the nettle and went ahead with the project as a private venture. It was not the last time that the foresight of the Hawker directors would prove invaluable to British national interest. Dr. Percy Walker, a designer at Hawker's from 1933 to 1935, commented: "As a private venture, the design from the beginning was subject to certain limitations, mainly owing to the need to control cost. The firm were compelled to apply existing design techniques to their monoplane, and make use of existing machine tools and workshop methods. . . . This meant a structure composed mainly of steel tubes and covered with fabric. The use of fabric for wing-covering produced a problem which was far from easy. By the standards of the time, the speed of the Hurricane was very high indeed, much faster than any of its biplane predecessors. Never before had fabric wing-covering been subject to such speeds and loading for any length of time."

Camm and his design team began working on the Fury Monoplane in the spring of 1933. The first design envisaged what was essentially a Fury fuselage fitted with a single low wing of 38-foot span. It had a fixed, spatted under-carriage and was powered by a Rolls-Royce Goshawk of 660 hp. Top speed was estimated at 280 mph, which compared very favorably with the 203 mph of the Fury.

The Hurricane prototype (K5083) was rolled out in November 1935.

THE INTERCEPTOR MONOPLANE

Early in 1934, Rolls-Royce revealed that development work had started on a 12-cylinder, liquid-cooled engine under the designation PV-12. Its power-to-weight ratio promised a significant improvement over the Goshawk, and it was intended to produce at least 1,000 hp. The time and effort invested by Rolls-Royce during the preparation of the "R" engines for Supermarine's Schneider Trophy racers were paying dividends. Camm decided that incorporating the PV-12 would be sensible, even though it would mean considerable design changes in the new fighter. Since the changes meant that the direct link with the Fury would become more tenuous, the project became known simply as the Hawker Interceptor Monoplane.

The Hurricane prototype (K5083) in flight with test pilot George Bulman at the controls.

Air Ministry officials examined the Hawker design studies and, suitably impressed by their promise, issued Specification F.36/34, which was essentially written for the Hawker design. With Hitler now firmly in power and Germany committed to rearmament, the need for the RAF to re-equip with modern aircraft was pressing. At last, on 21 February 1935, the Air Ministry awarded Hawker a contract for: "One high-speed monoplane, Serial K5083, to the design submitted on 4 September 1934, and to be known as the F.36/34 single-seat fighter."

FLESH ON THE BONES

The first problem confronting the Hawker design team in the early stages was whether they should make the leap to such modern techniques as stressed-skin construction immediately or rely for the time being largely on the methods that had served them well in the past. It was decided that the need to produce quick results was paramount, and that it would therefore be best to avoid any changes requiring a lengthy learning process or the need for more new jigs and tools on the factory floor than were absolutely necessary. The old methods, it was believed, would suffice to create the fighter needed while holding down the costs of development.

The design took shape, built up on established concepts modified as necessary to meet the demands of a fast monoplane. The steel-tube longerons at the heart of the fuselage were surrounded by a secondary structure of wooden formers and stringers covered by fabric from the tail to the cockpit. The covering from there forward was of light metal panels. The new PV-12 engine (soon to be named Merlin) was firmly mounted on steel tubes, but the task of converting the Merlin's power into thrust was provided, in the beginning, by a simple two-bladed wooden propeller. Apart from a narrow area of metal close to the roots, the cantilever wings were fabric covered. The ailerons were of fabric, but the split trailing-edge flaps had duralumin covering. The undercarriage was retractable, and Camm

elected to have it retracting inwards, so ensuring that the fighter would have a wide stance on the ground, and therefore be more forgiving in operation on rudimentary airfields. This would be in contrast to its contemporaries, the Spitfire and the Bf109, both of which would have narrow-track, outward-retracting undercarriages. The Bf109, in particular, was to build itself an unenviable record of landing and taxiing accidents, largely attributable to the malevolent nature of its close-set wheels.

One year after starting construction at Kingston, K5083 was delivered by road to the Hawker assembly shed at Brooklands. Less than two weeks later it made its appearance as a complete aircraft. The first flight was made from Brooklands on 6 November 1935, with test pilot PWS "George" Bulman in the cockpit. (PWS Bulman had

The first production Hurricane (L1547) served for many months as a test aircraft at Brooklands. Transferred to the RAF during the Battle of Britain, it was eventually lost on 10 October 1940 while flying with No. 312 (Czech) Squadron.

difficulty remembering people's names and had the habit of referring to everyone male as George. He thereby became known as George.) He reported himself well satisfied, saying that the aircraft handled perfectly and had no apparent vices. Another Hawker test pilot, Philip Lucas, wrote: "We found the aeroplane easy to fly, stable in flight and on the ground, and with a much better view than anything we had flown before."

Three months later, the initial series of company tests having been completed and a speed of 325 mph at 16,500 feet having been achieved, K5083 was delivered to the Aeroplane and Armament Experimental Establishment (A&AEE) at Martlesham Heath for evaluation by Royal Air Force pilots. The service trials report issued at the completion of this stage emphasized the prototype's viceless handling qualities and praised the generally well balanced controls. Takeoff distance in a 5-mph headwind was 265 yards, and a landing from 50 feet on the approach, touching down at 70 mph, took 475 yards. In the climb, 15,000 feet was reached 5.7 minutes after takeoff, and 20,000 feet less than 3 minutes later. The service ceiling was 35,400 feet. The detailed figures contained in the report also confirm that K5083 was the first fighter aircraft in the world to exceed 300 mph in level flight. The only obvious RAF criticism drew attention to the increasing heaviness of the rudder and ailerons as higher speeds were attained. As is the case with any prototype, there were improvements to be

aircraft by agreeing in March 1936 that production should be initiated ahead of contract, with a policy to plan tooling and facilities for 1,000 aircraft. . . . This early board decision gave a lead of considerable importance in the light of subsequent events."

It has sometimes been argued that this step cut short the further development of the fighter and prevented the addition of improvements that might have raised the aircraft's performance to a level closer to that of its principal adversary, the Bf109. However, Bert Tagg's closing comment seems nearer the heart of the matter. As the aviation historian Francis K. Mason has written, "It has been estimated that had the Hurricane been delayed for development as long as the Spitfire, Fighter Command would have taken delivery of some 600 fewer Hurricanes than it did by August 1940." A shortfall of that magnitude could well have proved fatal to the RAF during the Battle of Britain, thus clearing the way for Hitler to achieve complete success on his western front. Such an eventuality would surely have led to a marked shift in the course of world history.

PRODUCTION AND DELIVERY BEGIN

The Air Ministry appeared to be as keen as Hawker's to get on with the job of producing fighters. Only three months after the Hawker board decision, on 3 June 1936, a contract was awarded to the company for 520 aircraft. Production drawings were issued to the factory within a

No. 111 Squadron's Hurricanes lined up at RAF Northolt in 1938. The Hawker Hart used by George Bulman, the Hawker test pilot, is in the background.

made, but it was encouraging for the RAF to know that there was now a fighter that had a marked speed advantage over the bombers being produced for the recently created Luftwaffe.

The favorable reports from Martlesham Heath were followed by rumors that the Air Ministry was likely to recommend volume production of the new fighter. At this point, the Hawker directors once again showed the courage of their convictions. Bert Tagg, a member of Hawker's production staff from 1935 onward, recalled the event: "The Hawker directors demonstrated their confidence in the

week, and on 27 June the F.36/34 at last lost the anonymity of being a mere number and gained the distinction of a name – Hurricane. In July, Hurricane prototype K5083 made its public debut to great acclaim at the Hendon Air Display, where it was flown by A&AEE test pilot Squadron Leader Anderson.

Given the scale of production required, it was soon clear that Hawker's facilities at Kingston and Brooklands would not be adequate. In 1934, Hawker's had acquired the Gloster Aircraft Company, which from 1938 on was charged with the volume production of Hurricanes. In 1936 a new factory was constructed at Langley, just west of London, which also began delivering Hurricanes in 1938. These measures were timely, since a further contract for 1,000 fighters was issued in November 1938. Later on, from mid-1940, Hurricanes were also being built by the Canadian Car and Foundry Company in Montreal. (Canadian-built Hurricanes were designated Mark Xs. They were powered by Merlins built under license by the Packard Motor Corporation in the United States.) By March 1941, twelve Hurricanes per day were being turned out by the UK factories, and an additional ten a week were arriving from Canada. Air Ministry production plans showed that Hurricanes averaged 10,300 man-hours to build, which compared to 15,200 man-hours for the Spitfire and was an indication of the advantages gained by having one of the two principal front-line fighters manufactured to a relatively simple design.

Canadian-built Hurricane X at the RAF Fighter Leaders' School in 1942.

Despite all the foresight and urgency displayed by Hawker's and the Air Ministry in 1936, there was one major item that caused some delay in the completion of the first production aircraft. The Merlin I engine in K5083 had teething troubles, which caused anxieties over its reliability. It was decided to wait for the improved Merlin II, and this meant that the first production Hurricane I, serial L1547, did not fly until 12 October 1937. After that, however, the pace quickened. The first Hurricane (L1548) was delivered to a front-line squadron, No. 111 at RAF Northolt, on 15 December, and five more followed before the end of the year. With the squadron fully equipped early in 1938, the commanding officer, Squadron Leader John Gillan, did a bit of flag-waving. On 10 February, he set out to show that the Hurricane had an impressive turn of speed by flying from

Northolt to Turnhouse, near Edinburgh, a distance of 327 miles, in less than one hour. At first, it seemed unfortunate that he had chosen a day when an exceptionally strong northerly wind was blowing. Flying at full throttle all the way, he landed at Turnhouse well over an hour later, having averaged a less than notable 280 mph. He had planned to return to base the following day, but it occurred to him that the wind could be an asset if he refueled and went back immediately. This he did, touching down at Northolt just forty-eight minutes after taking off. Ignoring the northbound half of his flight and the contribution of the helpful tailwind, the Air Ministry announced that the Hurricane had averaged 409 mph from Edinburgh to London. The news raised a few German eyebrows and convinced most of the British public that the RAF had a 400-mph fighter. When his fellow pilots learned the facts of the matter, they nicknamed Gillan "Downwind," a burden he bore for the rest of his RAF career.

THE HURRICANE I

As delivered to the RAF, the early Hurricane Is still had fixed-pitch, two-bladed wooden propellers, but the engine bay had been modified to accept the Merlin II, giving the production aircraft a slightly different silhouette from the prototype. The overall dimensions of the airframe, however, were the same – wingspan 40 feet, length 31 feet. The foremost quarter of the fuselage was entirely taken up by the Merlin-filled engine compartment. Behind that came an armor-plated firewall, the reserve fuel tank (28 gallons), and then the cockpit, topped by a bullet-proof windscreen and a sliding canopy, which was eventually made jettisonable as well. The pilot's seat was backed by a sheet of armor. A spade-grip control column was fitted with the gun-firing button and the lever for the pneumatic brakes. The undercarriage and flaps were lever selected and hydraulically operated. Besides the usual red and green undercarriage lights indicating up and down, the Hurricane had the novel feature of two small windows in the cockpit floor through which the pilot could see the wheels when they were up. There were manual trimming controls for the elevator and rudder, and a standard flying instrument panel, together with an assortment of instruments to indicate the state of the fuel, electrical, pneumatic and hydraulic systems. Two 33-gallon self-sealing fuel tanks were fitted either side of the fuselage center section, and the armament of eight .303-in machine guns was mounted in two banks of four in the wings outboard of the undercarriage, so as to fire outside the propeller arc. Behind this concentration of equipment and services around the aircraft's center, the rear fuselage was left practically empty, serving only as the structure that carried the tail. In full fighting trim, complete with pilot, the Hurricane I weighed some 6,600 pounds.

Early and much-needed modification of the Hurricane I included such apparently minor adjustments as adding a small ventral strake underneath the rear fuselage to ease spin recovery, and connecting the static port of the altimeter to the air outside the cockpit. Modest though the altimeter modification seemed, it followed three fatal high-speed crashes on No. 111 Squadron and an incident that came close to ending the career of Hawker test pilot Philip Lucas. He later described letting down at speed into low cloud with the tops at 2,000 feet – according to his altimeter. "Almost immediately," he said, "I skimmed through the top of a wood, removing most of the fabric from the underside of the wings and fuselage." He managed to land safely at Kenley airfield, and put his fright down to misreading the altimeter. However, further investigation showed that when a Hurricane was diving at 400 mph, the altimeter reading could lag behind the aircraft by as much as 1,800 feet. The reason, as Lucas explained, was that "We had never flown before with enclosed cockpits, and our altimeters were just bolted to the instrument panel with the static pressure connection open to the cockpit, which obviously was at less than the local atmospheric pressure." When the instrument was connected to external static pressure, the troubling accidents ceased.

By 1939, stressed-skin metal wings were being manufactured. Roy Dutton, who was to become a Hurricane ace during the Battle of Britain, recalled that at high speed in the early aircraft, "the wing gun bay panels sometimes partially blew out and the wing fabric distended like sausages between the ribs." The new metal wings were much lighter and were stronger and stiffer in both bending and torsion. Inside the wings, a particularly significant change was the fitting of heating units for the guns. At the time of the Munich crisis in 1938, Hurricanes could not fire their guns above 15,000 feet because the mechanisms froze.

A modification vital to improving performance was to be the replacement of the two-bladed wooden propeller. As an interim solution, a Hamilton three-bladed metal propeller with two pitch settings was introduced. This was far from ideal because, though takeoff was much quicker, its performance at height was hardly any better than its wooden predecessor and it sprayed oil onto the windscreen. A constant-speed unit was tried, but the oil problem continued and the unit responded only slowly to rapid movements of the throttle. It was not until Rotol constant-speed propellers were introduced that the Hurricane made the most of its potential. At the same time, Rolls-Royce had discovered that by pointing the Merlin's exhaust stubs to the

rear instead of at right angles to the slipstream an increase in thrust could be achieved. This added some 5 mph to the average Hurricane's maximum speed, and "ejector exhausts," as they were called, were fitted to all Merlin engines from then on.

Generally speaking, the Hurricane was considered an easy aircraft to fly. Initial fears that the average RAF pilot would find it something of a handful, because its performance was so much more impressive than anything they might have flown before, were unfounded. In his later years, Air Marshal Sir Richard Atcherley, a member of the RAF's 1929 Schneider Trophy team, remembered that, to start with, new pilots were instructed to "fly the first few sorties in the Hurricane with the undercarriage down, because it went so bloody fast with it up!" By the standards of the jet age, such

Hurricane IIC (BD867) of No. 3 Squadron at Hunsdon in September 1941. This was when the squadron began night operations. (Note the exhaust shields mounted in front of the cockpit.)

measures may seem ludicrous, but they are an indication of the nervousness of some RAF senior officers in the 1930s in making the leap from the familiar open-cockpit biplane, with all its drag-producing wires and protuberances, to the more powerful, all-enclosed, streamlined monoplane.

Takeoff in the Hurricane was straightforward. There was a natural tendency for the fighter to swing, but this was easily checked with rudder. If there was a problem, it came after lifting off, and then only for the neophyte's early sorties. The throttle was conventionally positioned on the left, but

Hurricane IIAs of No. 71 "Eagle" Squadron in 1941.

with a Merlin III engine and a Rotol propeller, and flying at an all-up weight of 6,400 pounds, he achieved a level speed of 345 mph at 15,000 feet. Doubtless this sort of accomplishment did wonders for the export market. Impressed by the performance figures, a number of countries placed orders for Hurricanes – Persia, Turkey, Finland, Romania, and South Africa among them.

INTO BATTLE

When hostilities began in Europe on 1 September 1939 with the German invasion of Poland, the RAF was still well below the strength it was believed would be needed to defend the United Kingdom. By the end of that month, some 600 Hurricane Is had been manufactured, but barely half of them had been delivered to the front-line squadrons. Eighteen Hurricane and ten Spitfire squadrons were operational. Even when the few disastrously ineffective Defiant turret-fighter squadrons were added, this left a figure far short of the agreed estimate of fifty-two squadrons of modern fighters needed to defend Britain against a determined assault by the Luftwaffe.

Within hours of Britain's declaration of war on Germany, the decision was taken to send a British Expeditionary Force to France. Air support for the force consisted of Bristol Blenheim and Fairey Battle light bombers, and their protection was entrusted to four squadrons of Hurricanes, all of them early fabric-covered models fitted with two-bladed wooden propellers. On 9 September 1939, the squadrons landed in France; Nos. 1 and 73 were based at Octeville and Nos. 85 and 87 at Rouen. Two squadrons of obsolete Gladiator biplane fighters, Nos. 607 and 615, were sent to France as well, and they began re-equipping with Hurricanes during the spring of 1940. The excitement and bustle of these early days led to some expectation of vigorous early action, but it was not to be. An uneasy period of waiting for the next major German move began, popularly known as the Phoney War. It was a time of feints and skirmishes, of wondering when and where the blow would finally fall.

First blood for the Hurricanes in France was drawn on 30 October 1939 when Pilot Officer Peter "Boy" Mould,

the undercarriage lever was to the right. This meant that the pilot had to change hands on the stick to get the wheels up, a maneuver that almost invariably led new boys to "yo-yo" as they climbed away. That challenge coped with, a Hurricane pilot could reach 5,000 feet in two minutes and 15,000 feet in six and a half minutes. It took some thirteen minutes to reach 25,000 feet, and the service ceiling was 35,000 feet. At cruising speeds, the controls were light and responsive, but the ailerons became noticeably heavier at higher speeds. Landing was a relatively simple matter, though the Hurricane's speeds were higher than the Fury's, which initially suggested that getting it back on the ground might be difficult. Nothing could have been further from the truth. The wheels were lowered downwind at 150 mph, and the final approach was made at 90 mph, with a benign touchdown occurring for most pilots at about 70 mph. Pilot Officer Roland "Bee" Beamont, who was posted to France to join 87 Squadron in October 1939, having accumulated a total of 130 flying hours, has said: "To a newcomer the Hurricane was an immensely powerful but not very demanding aeroplane. Its wide-track undercarriage, stable and responsive flying characteristics, and reliable engine and hydraulic system resulted in a general atmosphere of confidence on the squadron, so that the newcomer had no reason to become apprehensive."

Although the maximum speed for the production Hurricane Mark I was given as 316 mph at 17,500 feet, in February 1939, test pilot George Bulman set a Hurricane speed record in a civilian-registered aircraft (G-AFKX). Fitted

the youngest member of No. 1 Squadron, shot down a Dornier 17 west of Toul. Other successes followed at intervals, but the curtain did not rise on the main event until the late spring of 1940. On 10 May, German forces began their western offensive. The Luftwaffe launched massive attacks on Allied airfields and gave strong support to the German Army's advance into Holland, Belgium and France. Fighting in the air was fierce, with the Hurricane squadrons heavily involved. At the end of the day, many of the RAF fighter pilots had flown six or seven combat sorties and all of them had seen furious action. By 12 May, there were ten Hurricane squadrons operating in France, and the equivalent of two more followed the next day. Though it was slower than its Luftwaffe counterpart, the Bf109, there were times when the Hurricane's rugged construction and great maneuverability were much appreciated by its pilots. One of the RAF commanders in France, Group Captain Fullard, wrote: "I have never seen squadrons so confident of success, so insensible to fatigue and so appreciative of their aircraft." "Bee" Beamont of 87 Squadron was one pilot who was particularly grateful for his fighter's turning abilities during an attack on a German bomber formation: "We closed in on the Dorniers and I hit one pretty hard. I suddenly noticed some stuff coming down past me like bright rain. It was tracer bullets. There was a Messerschmitt 110 very close, doing a tight attack on me from above. I didn't know what I was doing. I hadn't the slightest idea, except that I thought if I'm under fire from a fighter the thing to do was pull that aeroplane of mine into the tightest possible turn, which I did. I got a view of that 110 diving away out of sight."

On 14 May, with the German advance proving irresistible, a desperate French government asked for another ten Hurricane squadrons. Although Churchill was shocked by the French collapse and wished to help, he was given pause by the power of Air Chief Marshal Sir Hugh Dowding's argument that such valuable assets would be lost in trying to stave off an inevitable French defeat. As Commander-in-Chief of RAF Fighter Command, Dowding was responsible for Britain's first line of defense. In the course of one of the most remarkable letters ever signed by a British C-in-C, Dowding wrote to the Under-Secretary of State for Air on 16 May: "I must point out that within the last few days the equivalent of ten squadrons have been sent to France, that the Hurricane

squadrons remaining in this country are seriously depleted, and that the more squadrons which are sent to France the higher will be the wastage and the more insistent the demand for reinforcements.... If the Home Defence Force is drained away in desperate attempts to remedy the situation in France, defeat in France will involve the final, complete and irremediable defeat of this country."

Even so, Churchill sought for a way to satisfy the French government by reinforcing the fighters in France, eventually agreeing to the compromise solution of having some of the squadrons based in England flying to France for operations each day. This was to little avail. By 21 May, it was all over and the RAF began withdrawing from France, leaving behind most of its ground equipment, together with those aircraft that could not be made serviceable to fly. Among the recovery efforts made, none was more remarkable than that of Pilot Officer Louis Strange, a former WWI RFC pilot sent to organize the recovery of Hurricanes from

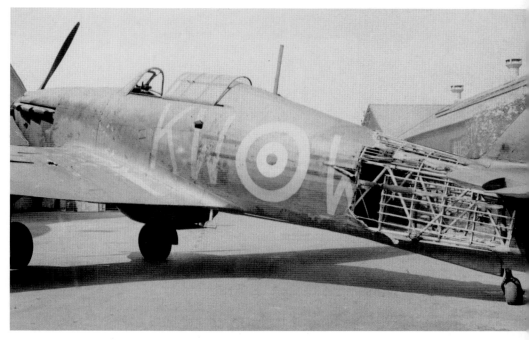

The Hurricane of Pilot Officer A. J. J. Truran, No. 615 Squadron, safely back at RAF Kenley after being struck by cannon fire from a Messerschmitt Bf109 on 15 August 1940.

Merville. He found himself with just one barely serviceable aircraft left, but with nobody to fly it. Fifty years old and never having flown anything like a Hurricane before, he decided to take it back to England himself. He managed to shake off the attentions of several Bf109s during the Channel crossing and then reached RAF Manston, where he landed safely, demonstrating both the continued excellence of his piloting skills and the obliging nature of the Hurricane.

The evacuation of Allied troops from Dunkirk began on 26 May, and during the week which followed nearly

350,000 men were taken off the beaches and from the port. RAF fighters flew almost 3,000 sorties in support of the operation, which ended on 4 June. For the first time, the Luftwaffe was confronted by RAF Fighter Command in strength and the air fighting was intense. The ferocity of the struggle was captured by Flight Lieutenant R. D. G. Wight, a Hurricane pilot of No. 213 Squadron, in a letter home: "Well, another day is gone and with it a lot of grand blokes. Got another brace of 109s today, but the whole of the Luftwaffe seems to leap on us – we were hopelessly outnumbered. I was caught napping by a 109 in the middle of a dogfight and got a couple of holes in the aircraft, one of them filled the office with smoke, but the Jerry overshot and he's dead." (Wight was himself killed in action two months later.)

Sea Hurricane IBs of No. 801 Squadron on board an Illustrious-class aircraft carrier in 1942.

Nearly 200 Luftwaffe aircraft were destroyed over Dunkirk, at a cost of over 100 RAF fighters and eighty of their pilots. In all, the Battle of France cost the Luftwaffe some 1,300 aircraft of all types, while the RAF lost nearly 950, of which 453 were single-seat fighters (386 Hurricanes and 67 Spitfires), the equivalent of over twenty-eight squadrons. A large proportion of the Hurricanes had not been destroyed in combat. They had been under repair at the time of the RAF withdrawal and had been abandoned. Perhaps even more serious than the loss of aircraft was the fact that 320 British pilots had been killed and 115 more imprisoned, among them some eighty squadron and flight commanders. At this stage of the war, moreover, the Luftwaffe appeared to be better placed to restore its front line than its opponent, and as

Britain prepared for the forthcoming aerial onslaught, RAF Fighter Command felt that it had been cut to the bone.

The situation had not been helped by the brief but disastrous intervention of British forces in Norway. During this campaign, No. 263 Squadron (Gladiators) and No. 46 Squadron (Hurricanes) were taken across the Norwegian Sea by aircraft carrier and deployed ashore to operate in support of surface forces near Narvik. Between them, they flew 638 combat sorties and claimed thirty-seven enemy aircraft destroyed, but it was soon apparent that their efforts were in vain. The remaining eight Gladiators were recovered by HMS *Glorious* and orders were received to destroy the Hurricanes. However, the 46 Squadron pilots volunteered to attempt carrier landings and the Hurricanes were flown out to the *Glorious*. All ten fighters were brought safely aboard in the first deck landings ever made by their pilots. Their brave efforts went for naught, however, when on 8 June 1940 the *Glorious* was sunk by gunfire from the German battle cruisers *Scharnhorst* and *Gneisnau*. Along with the ship and most of her crew, all the precious Hurricanes were lost, as were all but two of the pilots. One of the lessons learned from the disaster, however, was that doubts about operating modern monoplane fighters from ships were unfounded.

BRITAIN AT BAY

The fall of France shocked and saddened the British nation. However, once it became a fact of life, it could be seen that the problems of the war with Germany were greatly simplified, especially for the RAF. Dowding reacted to the news of French capitulation by saying "Thank God we are now alone." Disturbed though he was by the French defeat, Dowding now knew that his forces would no longer be drawn away and lost in a battle of attrition before meeting their primary duty of defending Britain. As it was, he knew that Fighter Command was very thinly spread. On the morning of 5 June, there were only 331 serviceable Hurricanes and Spitfires, with just thirty-six more in immediate reserve.

By the time the Battle of Britain began (officially recognized as 10 July 1940, though there was heavy skirmishing throughout the period following the fall of France), the situation had changed and Hitler's chances of subduing the recalcitrant British had diminished considerably. Fighter Command's order of battle on that day showed thirty-one Hurricane squadrons and nineteen Spitfire squadrons on strength. Together with the two Defiant squadrons, they made up the fifty-two squadrons that Dowding considered the minimum needed to confront the Luftwaffe with any hope of success. However, it must be remembered that not all of these squadrons were fully operational from the outset.

Many of the Hurricane squadrons, in particular, having borne the brunt of the fighting in France, were still recovering. No. 73 Squadron, for example, had been sent north to Church Fenton in Yorkshire on its return to England, where it licked its wounds in what was supposed to be a quiet sector, well away from the principal threat across the narrow waters of the English Channel. As it settled in to its new base, No. 73 reported only seven pilots fit for operations. All of its aircraft were in need of repair to some extent, and more than half of the ground crew were assumed to be still finding their way back from France. For a while, several other Hurricane squadrons were in a similar state.

The Battle of Britain can be divided into five phases. Between 10 July and 7 August, the Luftwaffe attacked coastal targets and convoys in the Channel. Fighter formations trailed their coats off the English coast in attempts to draw RAF Fighter Command into a battle of attrition. Dowding was not to be tempted, however. RAF squadrons were ordered to avoid combat with German fighters whenever possible. The fighters, after all, were not the main threat, and the RAF needed to conserve its strength for the trial to come, when bombers would be the priority targets. Even so, a number of actions were fought in which both sides learned some hard lessons. The RAF began to discover that its old-fashioned battle formation tactics were dangerously out of date, and the Defiant turret-gun fighter was an anachronism that did not belong in combat against Messerschmitt Bf109s. The Luftwaffe became similarly disillusioned about the twin-engined Messerschmitt Bf110. In the second phase, from 8 to 23 August, the Luftwaffe began to attack mainland targets, striking principally against RAF Fighter Command and the British aircraft industry. The first raids of the main assault were launched on 13 August, the day declared by Reichsmarschall Goering as "Adlertag" (Eagle Day). At this point he was still confident that he could defeat RAF Fighter Command in four days. Since this did not happen, Luftwaffe operations were intensified during the third phase, from 24 August to 6 September, in a determined effort to break the back of the opposition.

By early September, both sides were showing signs of strain and had suffered heavy casualties, but the RAF was still intercepting the Luftwaffe's raids and inflicting heavy losses on its enemies. Surprisingly, the Germans never solved the mysteries of the British defense system, failing to grasp the significance of radar and how it was used to control the RAF's fighters to such good effect. A turning point was reached in the Battle on 7 September, when the fourth phase began with the Luftwaffe making London its principal target. Fighter escort for the bomber formations was increased in strength. From then until the end of the month, the bombing

Pilots of No. 601 "County of London" Squadron scrambling during the Battle of Britain.

attacks were aimed both at breaking the spirit of the British capital and at destroying RAF Fighter Command in air battles with the massive fighter escort. In fact, the move relieved the pressure on the hard-pressed RAF stations, and Fighter Command was able to rebuild. By 15 September (Battle of Britain Day), it had become clear that the Luftwaffe's assault had failed, though daylight bomber raids continued sporadically for another two weeks. During the month of October, the fifth phase of the Battle, the Luftwaffe effectively abandoned its attempt to defeat the RAF, resorting to launching pinprick raids by fighter-bombers and diverting the main bomber force to a campaign of night raids.

A surprising postscript to the Battle of Britain was added on 11 November 1940 when the Italian Air Force carried out its only raid in strength against England. Hurricanes of 46, 249 and 257 Squadrons intercepted and shot down seven of the ten Fiat BR20 bombers involved plus four of the forty CR42 fighters that escorted them.

HURRICANE ACHIEVEMENT

From the beginning to the end of the Battle of Britain, the RAF's Hurricane squadrons were at the heart of the struggle. Without Sydney Camm's warhorse, the Battle could not have been won. On average, Hurricanes formed two-thirds of the strength of Fighter Command throughout, and they accounted for a similar proportion of the 1,733 Luftwaffe aircraft destroyed. There were 915 RAF fighters lost. (The figures given for losses are those from the RAF's official history. Other interpretations of the records have arrived at different totals, but none suggest significant variations in the comparison between the two air forces. Aircraft damaged are not included in either total. Note also that the figures take account of only those forces directly involved in the Battle. RAF losses in other operations have not been counted.)

Group Captain Dennis David, with the Hurricane I at the RAF Museum, Hendon.

By 30 October 1940, there were thirty-four Hurricane squadrons on the strength of Fighter Command, including one Canadian, two Czech and two Polish squadrons. Two more Polish squadrons were working up. No. 303 (Polish) Squadron had been declared operational in August and became the most successful RAF unit in the Battle, shooting down 127 Luftwaffe aircraft. No. 303's top-scoring pilot was in fact a Czech, Josef Frantisek, who was credited with seventeen victories during the month of September. He was killed in action on 8 October, one of 267 Hurricane pilots to lose their lives in the Battle of Britain.

HURRICANE PILOTS

During the Battle of France a number of RAF pilots began to show that they possessed a notable talent for aerial combat, and because of the way the squadrons had been deployed, they were all Hurricane pilots. Flying Officer "Cobber" Kain, a New Zealander flying with 73 Squadron, began his turbulent career by shooting down a Dornier 17 on 2 November 1939. The horrors of aerial combat were brought home to him when he landed and went to visit the crash site. Appalled to find the dismembered remains of the German crew lying

among the wreckage, he turned away, muttering, "Well – it was either them or me." Kain became the first RAF "ace" and had achieved sixteen victories by the time he was posted to become a flying instructor just before his squadron left France. Saying goodbye to his friends with a flourish, he was killed when he crashed during a low-level pass across 73 Squadron's airfield.

Flying Officer Dickie Lee, Flying Officer "Fanny" Orton, Pilot Officer Albert Lewis, and Pilot Officer Dennis David were prominent among those Hurricane pilots who scored multiple victories in the early days. Orton's total reached fifteen during the campaign in France before being wounded; he returned to operations but was killed in 1941. Lee, who raised his total to nine, was last seen chasing three enemy aircraft out over the English coast on 18 August. Both Lewis and David went on to further success. Lewis, a South African, produced a remarkable effort for 249 Squadron when, on 27 September, he destroyed six aircraft in one day – three Bf109s, two Bf110s and a Ju88. These gave him a total of eighteen, but they were his last. He was shot down on the following day and seriously burned.

Dennis David of 87 Squadron fought through both the Battles of France and Britain, achieving twenty-one aerial victories. He survived the war unscathed, flying both Spitfires and Beaufighters on operations and rising to the rank of Group Captain. In his book *Dennis "Hurricane" David* (Grub Street, 2000), David leaves no doubt of his respect and affection for the Hurricane. "I have waged a long campaign to get the Hurricane given its due as the major victor in the Battle of Britain," he writes. "Although today it is far less famous than the Spitfire, in fact Hurricanes shot down more enemy aircraft than all the Spitfires, anti-aircraft and other aircraft combined." He also recalls conversations with former Luftwaffe bomber airmen in which they confided that "the Hurricane was the aircraft they dreaded."

Among the most famous of all Hurricane pilots was Douglas Bader. He lost both legs in a flying accident in the early 1930s, but mastered artificial limbs and finally convinced the RAF that they could not do without him. He not only returned to operational flying but commanded No. 242 Squadron during the Battle of Britain. The guidance he gave his pilots was simple: "He who has the sun creates surprise. He who has the height controls the battle. He who gets in close shoots them down." Bader was an inspirational leader and a fighter pilot of great determination. He was officially credited with twenty-three victories by 9 August 1941, when he was forced to bail out of a stricken Spitfire during a dogfight over northern France, leaving one of his legs lodged in the cockpit. The German troops who took him prisoner were astonished to find that their captive

Dennis David once again in the cockpit of a Hurricane.

had one leg of his flying suit empty and the other filled with a mechanical device.

Peter Townsend took command of 85 Squadron in May 1940, rebuilding it after its withdrawal from France with the help of battle-hardened survivors such as Dickie Lee and Sammy Allard. In his book *Duel of Eagles* he mentions the new pilots: "They were boys of twenty and sometimes less, with only ten hours Hurricane experience. . . . We taught them to search the sky and watch their tails. They jousted with us in the sky to learn the tricks of air combat – above all never climb or dive in front of a 109, but turn and turn again, since it was there that the Hurricane outclassed the 109." When the Battle of Britain began, he had no doubt about his responsibilities: "We RAF fighters were not in the least interested in the German fighters – except insofar as they were interested in us. Our job was defence. German fighters could do no harm to Britain. German bombers with their deadly loads were the menace. Our orders were to seek them out and destroy them. Only when their 109 escort interfered did it become a fleeting battle between fighters. We tried to avoid them, not to challenge them." Townsend's preferred method of getting to the bombers quickly was the head-on attack, and he describes one he led on 26 August: "I brought the

squadron around steadily in a wide turn, moving it into echelon as we levelled out about two miles ahead on a collision course. Ease the throttle to reduce the closing speed – which anyway allowed only a few seconds fire. Get a bead on them right away, hold it, and never mind the streams of

Dennis David and an 87 Squadron fighter, 1940.

Michael Turner's painting of night operations in Hurricanes.

tracer darting overhead. Just keep on pressing on the [gun] button until you think you are going to collide – then stick hard forward. Under the shock of negative 'G' your stomach jumps into your mouth, dust and muck fly up from the cockpit floor into your eyes, and your head cracks on the roof as you break away below."

Townsend also mentions that the Luftwaffe fighter pilots were contemptuous about the Hurricane and preferred to believe that they were being shot down by Spitfires: "We thought [the Hurricanes] were great and would prove it by shooting down around 1,000 Luftwaffe aircraft in the Battle. The Luftwaffe airmen often mistook Hurricanes for Spitfires. . . . During the Battle of France, Theo Osterkamp (a celebrated Luftwaffe fighter leader) seemed to see Spitfires everywhere. There were no Spitfires in the Battle of France, only Hurricanes. Even General Kesselring said, 'Only the Spitfires bothered us.' The Luftwaffe seemed to be suffering from Spitfire snobbery."

Bob Stanford Tuck began the Battle of Britain flying Spitfires, and was not altogether happy when posted to take command of 257 Squadron, flying Hurricanes, in September

1940. He admitted to being "not very impressed" on his first inspection of the Hurricane, describing it as looking "like a great sturdy carthorse." However, during his first flight, he "became aware of its virtues," and after leading 257 into combat for the first time "my first impressions of this magnificent aircraft were completely wiped out, as I realized the sterling qualities of its handling. It had not a vice in its whole make-up. Its wonderful visibility over the nose, and its remarkable steadiness and solidness when the eight machine guns crashed into life made it an absolute delight to fly – but I would have liked more speed. I felt sure that if under heavy attack it was capable of taking tremendous punishment, and this later proved to be the case."

"Ginger" Lacey, Frank Carey, Mike Crossley, Gerry Edge, Archie McKellar, Witold Urbanowicz, Ian "the Widge" Gleed, "Darkie" Hallowes – these and many other Hurricane pilots distinguished themselves during the Battles of France and Britain. They were among the best-known airmen from the many countries who fought with the RAF in those perilous times – Britain, Canada, Australia, New Zealand, South Africa, Poland, Czechoslovakia, France, Belgium, Ireland,

Southern Rhodesia, and one each from Jamaica and Palestine. There were seven Americans, too, the first of whom to die was Billy Fiske, who succumbed to his wounds after landing his 601 Squadron Hurricane on fire at Tangmere on 16 August 1940. (Of the original "magnificent seven," only one, Ken Haviland, survived the war. In 1940, he flew Hurricanes with 151 Squadron.)

Also on that day in August, James Nicolson of 249 Squadron was involved in his first combat, an experience that brought him the only Victoria Cross ever awarded to a Fighter Command pilot. Nicolson was bounced by a Bf109 while patrolling over Southampton, and his Hurricane was hit by four cannon shells. Wounded in the face by shards of perspex from the shattered canopy and in the left foot by a shell, Nicolson was enveloped in flames erupting from the fuselage fuel tank. He started to abandon the aircraft, but then saw a Bf110 ahead of him. Dropping back into the seat, he brought his guns to bear and fired. He kept the gunsight on the Bf110 and continued firing as the flames peeled the flesh from his hands and scorched his face. Bailing out with some difficulty, he managed to pull the ripcord of his parachute with hands that had become little more than claws. He began to suffer agonies from his wounds, but his ordeal under fire was not over. As he neared the ground, some over-zealous Local Defence Volunteers mistook him for a Luftwaffe pilot and opened fire, hitting him in the buttocks with a charge of buckshot. Nicolson's reaction to the news of his Victoria Cross was, "Now I'll have to earn it."

HOURS OF DARKNESS

By the end of 1940, the basic Fury Monoplane design of the Hurricane was beginning to look a little dated. Improvements were on the way, however, and there were still many jobs left for the Hurricane to do. For example, as the Luftwaffe bombers, rebuffed by day, turned to a night offensive, some Hurricane squadrons were pressed into service in the night-fighting role. Peter Townsend's 85 Squadron was among the first. Since there was nothing about his aircraft that might be said to qualify them as night fighters, he was somewhat surprised. Admirable as the Hurricane had proved in its intended role as a day fighter, it was a single-seat, single-engined aircraft without radar or navigation aids. Its Merlin engine trailed highly visible tongues of blue flame from its exhausts, and the gunsight's brilliantly lit optics, so clear by day, were blindingly bright at night. No. 85 Squadron (together with other hastily adapted Hurricane units – 73, 87 and 151 Squadrons among them) flew many fruitless hours in the dark, patrolling endlessly in the hope of stumbling across the path of a raider. Contacts were few and

far between. On 27 October 1940, Sammy Allard intercepted a Luftwaffe aircraft as it attacked two RAF machines showing navigation lights. Lining up on his enemy's exhaust flames, Allard fired and was promptly blinded by his own tracers, so losing contact. On the following night, Geoff Goodman was startled when an enemy aircraft revealed itself

A Hurricane biplane! L1884 was fitted with a jettisonable upper wing as an experiment in generating more lift during takeoff from small, unimproved airfields. The upper wing could also have carried extra fuel to extend the aircraft's range.

by opening fire. He promptly fired back, only to lose his target as Allard had done. These brief and inconclusive contacts exemplified the problem of using the Hurricane as a defensive night-fighter. It was a "by guess and by God" operation, with pilots being left largely to their own devices, depending on initiative, instinct and pure chance. As more specialized night fighters such as the Beaufighter appeared, the Hurricane was gradually relieved of its nighttime frustrations.

IMPROVING THE BREED

In February 1940, Hawker's made their initial proposal for a Mark II variant of the Hurricane, powered by the Merlin XX engine, which was to be fitted with a two-stage supercharger producing 1,175 hp at 21,000 feet. An additional advantage was that the new engine was cooled by a seventy percent water/thirty percent glycol mixture, which, unlike the pure glycol previously used, was not inflammable. Armament was to be increased from eight to twelve .303-in machine guns. Approval for development was quickly given, and by June 1940 the prototype Mark II was in the air. Hawker's production of Mk IIs soon began, and they appeared in various guises thereafter. The Mk IIA retained the eight-gun wings, but the Mk IIB, which was produced from April 1941, had an increased armament of twelve machine guns. In the same month, the first Mk IICs were delivered to Nos. 3 and 257 Squadrons, and these carried four 20-mm cannon. Other modifications included providing tropical filters for aircraft going to overseas theatres, and hard points to allow the carriage of both fuel tanks and bombs under the wings. In 1942, the range of armament was widened to include

Soviet Hurricane IIA (Z5252) at Vaenga, near Murmansk.

40-mm cannon and unguided rockets. (The Hurricane was the first single-seat fighter of WWII to be armed with rockets.) When fitted with two 40-mm cannon, the Hurricane became the Mk IID and was known as "the tin-opener." Its maximum speed fell to 286 mph but, as its nickname suggests, it proved an invaluable weapon against armored vehicles. The final production version of the Hurricane was the Mk IV, which introduced the universal armament wing, capable of accepting 40-mm cannon, bombs, long-range tanks, or rockets as required. Intended solely for low-level attack operations, it was fitted with additional armor plate. In its heaviest form, the Hurricane's weight rose to well over 9,000 pounds.

Reverting temporarily to the appearance of its ancestors, a Hurricane Mk I was flown experimentally with a jettisonable upper wing. Doubtless that generated more lift

for takeoff, as was intended, but the idea was soon abandoned as impractical. In 1943, a Hurricane Mk V was flown, and two Mk IVs were modified to Mk V standard, fitted with the more powerful Merlin 32. Overheating problems brought about the Mk V project's cancellation. Other Mark numbers were allocated to Hurricanes built in Canada, the Marks X, XI and XII corresponding generally with their British counterparts. Most Canadian aircraft used Packard Merlins.

THE FAR FROZEN NORTH

Following the German attack on the Soviet Union in June 1941, Churchill promised Stalin that Britain would send aid, including aircraft. On 21 August, a convoy left Glasgow bound for Murmansk. It included the carrier HMS *Argus*, which had on board twenty-four partially assembled Hurricane Mk IIAs, with another fifteen packed in crates. The air and ground crews of Nos. 81 and 131 Squadrons went with them to establish the air defense of the Murmansk region and to train the Soviets to operate Hurricanes. This force was the vanguard of nearly 3,000 Hurricanes sent to the Soviet Union in the following three years.

The RAF squadrons moved onto Vayenga airfield and were ready for operations by 12 September. In the next few weeks, in steadily deteriorating weather conditions, they flew combat patrols, escorted Soviet bombing missions, and trained Soviet personnel. By the time they began handing over the aircraft over to the Soviets in mid-October, they had ably demonstrated the Hurricane's capabilities by shooting down fifteen enemy aircraft for the loss of one of their own. In recognition of their contributions, four RAF men were awarded the Order of Lenin; this was the only time any members of the Allied forces were so recognized in WWII. One Order of Lenin in particular was unique in that it was given to a non-commissioned officer. It was awarded to Sergeant "Wag" Haw, who had shot down three Bf109s in two weeks. An extract from one of Haw's reports shows how well he had learned the lessons of combat with Bf109s: "The leader of the [Bf109's] second section tried to do a beam attack on me, but I turned towards him and after three complete turns I was on his tail. I gave him several short bursts . . . as I fired the last burst but one, the enemy aircraft came out of its turn, climbed steeply, then stalled and went into a spin, white and black smoke pouring from it."

ALL AT SEA

When the Atlantic convoys, already threatened by U-boats, faced the added menace of long-range Luftwaffe aircraft, it was decided to convert a number of Hurricane Is to Mk IA Sea Hurricane standard and to operate them from modified merchant ships (Fighter Catapult Ships and Catapult Aircraft Merchantmen). It was a measure driven by desperation, because the idea was to catapult the Sea Hurricane (more colloquially known as a Hurricat) into the air when an enemy aircraft appeared, while having no means of recovering the fighter when its work was done. If the convoy was in range of land, all might be well; otherwise the pilot

A Sea Hurricane IA on the catapult of a CAM ship. The flaps are selected to the takeoff position.

could choose either to bail out or ditch near a ship. The first successful launch and interception occurred on 2 August 1941, when a FockeWulf Condor was shot down by Lieutenant Bob Everett flying from HMS Maplin, a Fighter Catapult Ship. In a total of 175 voyages undertaken with Hurricats, eight launches were made, resulting in the destruction of six enemy aircraft and the loss of one RAF pilot.

At the same time as the Hurricats were being sent to sea, the development of the Sea Hurricane went on. The aircraft was being reinforced for the fitting of arrester hooks. This was not an ideal solution since the Hurricane had never been thought of as a naval fighter. Test pilot Eric Brown described it as being "Short on range, with the ditching propensities of a submarine, harsh stalling characteristics, a very mediocre view for deck landing, and an undercarriage that was as likely as not to bounce it over the arrester wires." Nevertheless, from early 1941, the Fleet Air Arm began forming Sea Hurricane squadrons, first to be embarked on Fleet carriers such as HMS *Furious, Indomitable, Formidable,* and *Eagle.* Later, when the smaller escort carriers arrived, Sea Hurricanes went to sea in those, too. It was essentially an interim arrangement until supplies of American aircraft such as the Grumman Wildcat and Hellcat, specifically designed for carrier operations, became available. Nevertheless, the Sea Hurricanes of the Fleet Air Arm performed nobly until 1943, and were heavily involved in such actions as Operations Pedestal (the relief of Malta), the protection of the

Murmansk convoys, and Operation Torch (the Allied invasion of North Africa).

EUROPEAN CHALLENGES

In the summer of 1941 there were more than forty Hurricane squadrons based in the UK. (These included the three Eagle Squadrons, manned by pilots from the United States – Nos. 71, 121 and 133.) By the following summer that number had dwindled to a dozen. A newer generation of more capable aircraft had arrived, and many Hurricane units had been deployed to other theaters of war where the robust qualities of their aircraft would serve them well.

The change of momentum in the European air war after the Battle of Britain led RAF Fighter Command to move to the offensive. Hurricane squadrons, equipped with the various forms of Mk II, were involved both in escorting light bombers in raids across the Channel and in conducting fighter sweeps of their own. Some units took on intruder duties, penetrating enemy airspace at night to harass the Luftwaffe on and around its own bases, and adding night attacks on shipping for good measure. Among the most successful of the intruders was No. 1 Squadron based at Tangmere on England's south coast. The commanding officer, Squadron Leader James Mclachlan, had lost his left arm after being seriously wounded in an air battle over Malta in February 1941. Nevertheless, by November, he had returned to the front line as No. 1 Squadron's CO. He and his "A" Flight commander, a Czech named Karel Kuttelwascher, were implacable intruders, and in three months of intensive operations in 1942, they destroyed twenty of the twenty-two enemy aircraft shot down by the squadron, fifteen of them falling to the remarkable Czech.

During 1943, the replacement of Hurricanes in front-line squadrons based in the United Kingdom continued, but they remained valuable assets, assigned to such duties as operational training, meteorological reporting, target-towing and radar calibration. By the beginning of 1944, there were

James Nicolson, recipient of the only Victoria Cross awarded to a fighter pilot during WWII.

just three operational Hurricane squadrons left in the UK, and when D-Day dawned on 6 June 1944 there was only one, 309 Squadron, employed in the air defense of Scotland. Farther afield, Hurricanes remained at the point of the spear. As the Allies advanced north through Italy, the Balkan Air Force was formed to attack German positions in Yugoslavia in the summer of 1944. The Yugoslav-manned 351 Squadron, equipped with Mk IICs and Mk IVs, was prominent in providing air support for partisan forces operating against the Germans. Rocket-firing Hurricanes also flew from bases in Greece once the German troops withdrew northward.

INTERNATIONAL AFFAIRS

Italian forces entered Greece from Albania in October 1940; British military units were dispatched from Egypt to help in repelling the invasion. Initially, air defense was entrusted to 80 Squadron's Gladiators, but in early 1941, as German ele-

ments were brought into the struggle, the aging biplanes were exchanged for Hurricanes, and Nos. 33 and 208 Squadrons added theirs to the growing British force. During the winter months, the Allies engaged in a hopeless struggle against the inexorable Axis advance. The RAF was heavily outnumbered by the Regia Aeronautica and the Luftwaffe, and the aerial confrontation was savagely intense, the Hurricane squadrons being involved daily in fierce combat.

In the course of the campaign in Greece and Crete, the non-stop action produced some of the highest scoring Hurricane pilots of the war. Richard "Ape" Cullen of 80 Squadron achieved six kills in the Gladiator before undertaking a swift and informal conversion to the Hurricane in the front line at the end of February 1941. Five days later he was a Hurricane ace, having shot down a BR20, two SM79s and two CR42s in one day. Three days later he destroyed four enemy aircraft in one sortie, but on the following day he was bounced by several Fiat G50s and was not seen again. The combat record of 80 Squadron includes many more aces. William Vale achieved ten victories in the Gladiator; by the end of April, when the squadron had withdrawn to Crete, he had added another thirteen in the Hurricane. Four more followed in May before he was rested from operations. Ted Hewitt had sixteen kills, and Roald Dahl (the celebrated author of children's books) was also an 80 Squadron ace. The most outstanding figure of the campaign, however, was "Pat" Pattle, who first fought with the Gladiators of 80 Squadron before commanding 33 Squadron's Hurricanes. Remarkable by any standards, Pattle was described by a distinguished former squadron commander of his as being "of the bravest; an exceptional fighter leader and brilliant fighter pilot." With fifteen confirmed victories in the Gladiator, Pattle converted to the Hurricane in February 1941. His score mounted rapidly during March and April, including several instances of multiple kills in one day against such formidable opposition as the Luftwaffe's Bf109s. On 20 April, flying his third sortie of the day while suffering from influenza, he shot down two Bf110s. He was then seen going to the assistance of one of his flight commanders when he was in turn shot down and killed by fire from a Bf110. In the evacuation from Crete, 33 Squadron's records were lost, but it is clear that Squadron Leader Marmaduke Thomas St. John "Pat" Pattle was the highest scoring RAF fighter pilot of the war. The exact number of his victories will never be known, but some estimates have been as high as fifty-one, all of them after the first fifteen achieved in the Hurricane.

Further to the south and west, Hurricanes delivered under fire by aircraft carriers or flown in via the trans-African route after being shipped to the Gold Coast were heavily involved both in the defense of the vital island fortress of

Malta and in fighting against the Axis forces operating in North Africa. After considerable success against the Regia Aeronautica in the early desert campaigns, the Hurricane squadrons became increasingly associated with the land battle: the greater capabilities of the Mk IIs were used to advantage both for close support of Allied troops and in harassing enemy airfields and ground forces well beyond the front lines. In meeting the demands of the desert war, the Hurricane's versatility was repeatedly demonstrated. When fitted with two 40-mm cannon, it was the "tank-buster supreme," though this role was fraught with danger, and pilots of No. 6 Squadron reported "a marked loss of airspeed" when firing the guns. Hurricanes also continued as air-to-air fighters and operated as "Hurribombers," armed reconnaissance aircraft, and night fighters, besides performing anti-shipping strikes and convoy protection duties.

In the Far East, Hurricane Mk Is of No. 232 Squadron were among those unfortunate enough to experience the superiority of the Zero as Japanese forces enveloped Malaya, Singapore, and the East Indies. No. 17 Squadron was similarly pressed during the retreat from Burma. As the situation in the Far East stabilized and plans were made to drive the Japanese back, large numbers of new Hurricanes were brought into the theater; there were twenty-three squadrons (some 700 aircraft) available by June 1943, mostly Mk IIs but including some Mk IVs. With its excellent maneuverability and capacity to absorb punishment, the Hurricane was ideal for low-level operations over jungle. Once the Allied armies began taking the offensive in 1943, these often included such hazardous tasks as night attacks on ground targets. During the siege of Imphal, when much of the British 14th Army was surrounded, Hurricanes played an important part in keeping the Japanese at bay, striking heavily at enemy positions and helping to keep the skies clear of Japanese aircraft. No. 5 Squadron recorded the destruction of 705 enemy vehicles, ninety-eight river craft, twenty-nine tanks and four trains in the course of the Imphal battle.

By mid-'44, the number of Hurricane squadrons in the Far East had risen to thirty-seven, including several from the Indian Air Force, and it was the most numerous Allied aircraft in the theatre. Even though many units then began re-equipping with Spitfires and P-47 Thunderbolts, some Hurricanes were retained for ground-attack duties and eight squadrons (six from the IAF) were still operating in the front line at the end of the war.

When fulfilling their many roles in far-flung places, the Hurricanes, battle-scarred and often serviced by hard-pressed ground crew working with minimal maintenance facilities, flew and kept flying from desert strips, stony fields, rough pasture, beaches, or whatever reasonably clear space

A Hurricane IIB attacking a bridge on the Tiddim Road in Burma during the advance of the 14th Army against the Japanese in 1945.

was available. They flew in conditions that might be hot and dry or miserably wet and cold, the robust Hurricane undercarriage and rugged reliability allowing them to do so without undue complaint far longer than would have been the case with their more sophisticated cousins. They were indispensable assets in the pursuit of victory.

Hurricanes were with front-line squadrons on 1 September 1939 and were still serving when the Japanese surrendered in 1945, having fought on every front throughout WWII. In September 1944, the 12,950th and last Hurricane built in the United Kingdom was delivered. It was a Mark IIC named "The Last of the Many". A further 1,077 were built in Canada. Often overshadowed by their more glamorous contemporaries, the Hurricanes made major contributions to victory in every theater, none more vital than over Britain in the summer of 1940. Without them and their pilots, the foundations of Western civilization would have trembled.

"Bee" Beamont, one of Britain's most celebrated pilots, who flew with 87 Squadron during the Battle of Britain, recognized the sterling qualities of Sydney Camm's creation: "The Hurricane was a machine of its time, and many of us would not have changed it for any other mount. We knew it as a rugged, stable, forgiving aeroplane which was tolerant of our clumsiness and the worst that the weather could do. It absorbed legendary amounts of enemy fire and kept flying. We could hit the target well with its eight guns and when in trouble we felt that we could outfly the enemy's best."

Previous page: Sidney Camm's classic fighter atop an English hill. Nearby is a typical RAF fighter pilot's car, a 1927 Bentley. This Hurricane is in the colors of the famous fighter leader Douglas Bader.

Left: This fighter operated by the RAF (Battle of Britain Memorial Flight) is the last Hurricane of more than 14,000 built. For many years it carried the hand-painted inscription "The Last of the Many." A piece of the original fabric, removed during restoration, was rescued from a dustbin and is now framed and hung in a BBMF office.

Inset: Hurricane IIC (PZ865) "The Last of the Many."

Bottom: Douglas Bader, the famous legless fighter ace who commanded No. 242 Squadron of the Duxford Wing during the Battle of Britain.

From the rear quarter, the signature fin and rudder that denotes a Sidney Camm–designed airplane. Also obvious is the wood-and-fabric construction of the rear fuselage.

The large fin-flash as well as the dark earth and green camouflage signify the period of the Battle of Britain. The under fuselage fairing that surrounds the tail wheel was added after early Hurricanes proved difficult to recover from a spin.

The tailplane and the fittings for adjusting the rudder trim tab. Each elevator also included a trim tab, essential for fine-tuning a high-performance fighter in flight.

A Hurricane I receives attention from the skilled craftsman at Hawker Restorations. Visible here is the rugged construction that made the fighter so durable in the deadly skies of high-altitude combat. The legendary Rolls-Royce Merlin engine is surrounded by wires and tubing. The segmented opening in the leading edge of the wing is the front of the gun bay, which contained four .303-inch machine guns. The next opening contains a large landing light.

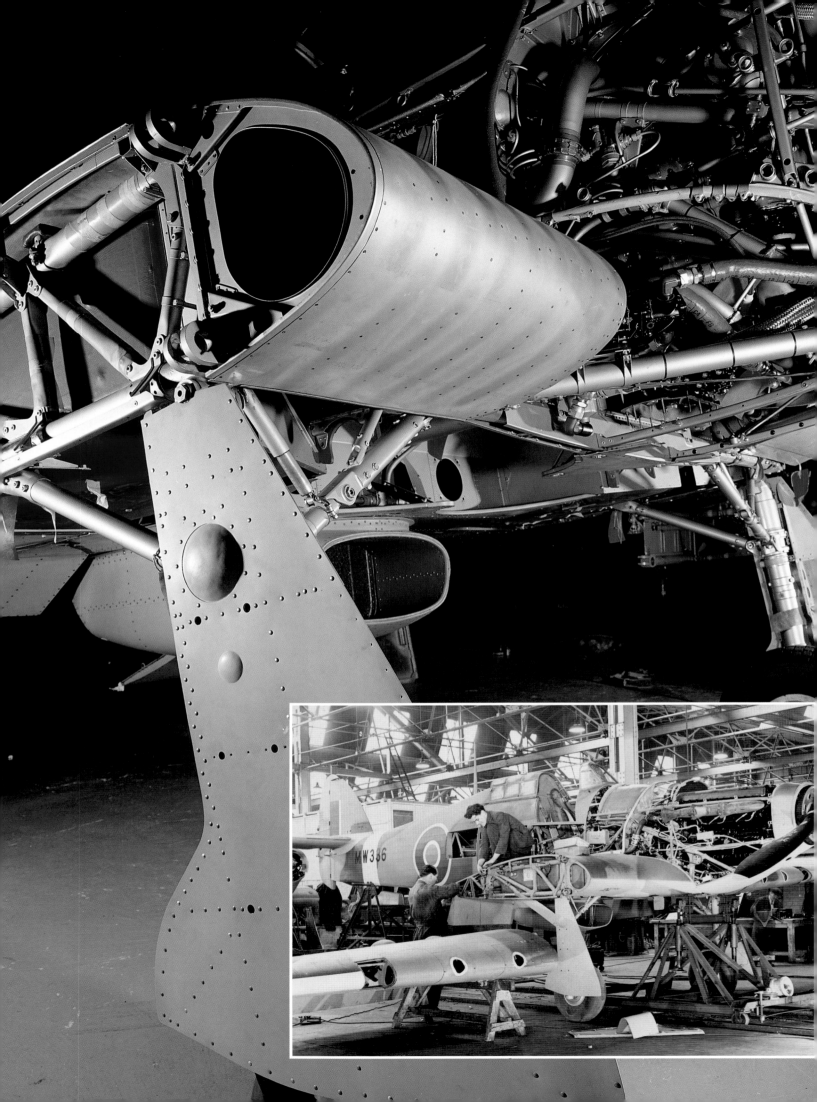

Left: The center section of a Hurricane is where the strength of the design is found. The undercarriage retracts inward. Here you can see the heavy construction that connects all the basic structures together, creating a very sturdy platform for an aerial weapon. Inside the wing structure, the red object is one of the fuel tanks.

Inset: Hurricanes under construction at Hawker's in 1944.

Top right: Underneath the wood-and-fabric shell, the tubular structure of the fighter is visible. This construction gave this airplane durability and the ability to survive heavy combat damage and keep flying. The very strong, light-weight tubing used by Hawker's was specially created in the 1930s and is no longer readily available. That is why so few Hurricanes have been restored to flying condition. Hawker Restorations researched the system and reproduced tubing to match that used by the manufacturers before WWII.

Bottom right: The tailplane, which is partially uncovered, shows the end of the central tubular structure. Tony Ditheridge, who owns and operates Hawker Restorations, explains that what Sidney Camm actually did was "figure out how to make a wooden airplane out of metal."

Top left: The wide stance of the fighter's undercarriage. This robust structure made the Hurricane very adaptable to all types of ground operations.

Bottom left: The large central radiator directly behind the wheel wells. Like all liquid-cooled engines, the Merlin was susceptible to gunfire, and damage to the cooling system meant that the powerful engine would soon seize up.

Top right: The flaps on the Hurricane are enormous and deploy to a staggering 89 degrees.

Bottom right: A Canadian-built Hurricane XII modified with skis and a snowshoe tail-unit. This aircraft has twelve-gun wings fitted and, as with most Canadian Hurricanes, there is no spinner on the Hamilton-Standard propeller.

During the Battle of Britain, engine maintenance was performed at all times at the dispersal as well as in the hangar. The uncowled Merlin is visible here. The heavy engine-mounts support the 1,320-lb motor. Behind the firewall the center fuel-tank is red.

Below: Armorers replenishing the gun bays of a Hurricane during the Battle of Britain.

Left: The BBMF Hurricane IIC has twelve separate exhaust stacks, one for each cylinder of the Merlin, an arrangement rarely seen on Hurricanes.

Top right: In the hangar, a Hurricane receives coolant in the header tank.

Right center: The Merlin's ejector exhaust stacks collected the gases of two cylinders each and added about 5 mph to the Hurricane's top speed.

Below right: The engine breather tubing is visible along the trailing edge of the left wing.

Top left: During the Battle of Britain, Hurricanes were fitted with eight .303 machine guns. Here the gun bay shows the arrangement of four guns. In early fighters, the guns froze and jammed at high altitude, so electric heaters were added. The ammunition was carried to the guns in tracks. These weapons carried enough bullets for about fifteen seconds of gunfire.

Top right: Later Hurricanes were fitted with 20-mm cannons. These heavy weapons delivered a withering fire that inflicted severe and often fatal damage to the structure of an opposing airplane.

Bottom right: Blisters were added to the upper wing-surface to accommodate the larger cannons.

Bottom left: A Hurricane IV fitted with a universal wing and carrying two 40-mm anti-tank guns.

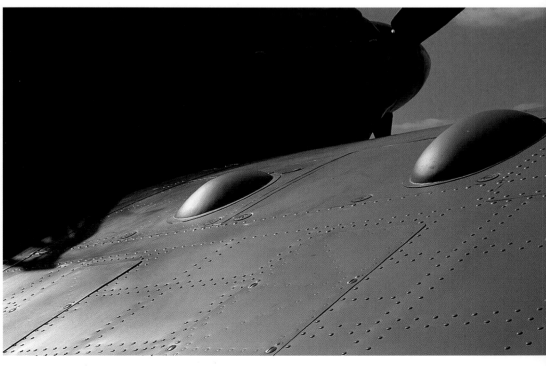

Left: Compared to the cockpit of a Spitfire, the Hurricane was roomy and comfortable. The metal bucket seat would have been filled with a seat-type parachute. At the pilot's left are the engine controls, just above the structural tubing that runs along the outer wall of the fuselage. The flying instruments are directly in front of the pilot and just below the gunsight. The distinctive "spade" grip of the control column and the gun button are at center. To the right of the pilot is the lever for raising and lowering the seat.

Top right: As the pilot climbs into his craft, this is his view of the long nose, which gently curves down toward the propeller. This design element gave the Hurricane pilot excellent visibility in combat. On top of the front windscreen is the rearview mirror, essential in aiding the pilot to see who or what was approaching him from behind.

Bottom right: A precursor of today's "heads up" display, the WWII gunsight. The sight projected a "pipper" onto the angled glass. The pilot then flew so as to place the "pipper" over his opponent's aircraft. The most successful pilots tried to get as close as possible to the enemy before firing, and fired only short bursts to conserve ammunition.

Top left: In the cockpit of the Hurricane. The pilot was closely confined, and all his combat tools were in front of him.

Bottom left: The pilot's right thumb rests on the button that fires the guns.

Right:The gunsight projected well into the cockpit and was fitted with padding intended to protect the pilot's head in the event of a forced landing. Nevertheless, the foreheads of many WWII fighter pilots bore scars, which seems to indicate that it did not work very well.

Bottom left: Robert Stanford Tuck in the cockpit of his Hurricane I. He commanded No. 257 (Burma) Squadron from the beginning of September 1940. In January 1942, when his victory total stood at twenty-nine, he was shot down in a Hurricane II during a fighter sweep over northern France and became a POW.

Before going onto alert, the fighter pilot would walk around his airplane to assure himself that it was ready for combat. The ground crews would have serviced the fighter and rearmed the guns, but the pilot must be satisfied that his aircraft is ready to do what he asks of it.

Left: A check of the rudder and trim tabs. The large rudder surface is also important for taxiing and ground operations, as the tailwheel is not steerable.

Top right: The ailerons are checked for full and free movement.

Bottom right: All access panels and wheel wells need the attention of the pilot.

Left: Dressed for high-altitude combat. The young pilots of the early 1940s were often rushed into combat with very little experience and just a few hours in the type of fighter they flew into battle. The green life vest was found to be very hard to spot in the waters of the English Channel. Many pilots painted theirs with any yellow paint they could find, until the Air Ministry started manufacturing them in yellow.

The Hawker Hurricane resting at dispersal at a forward English grass field, the camouflage matching the landscape.

Getting aboard the Hurricane takes a long step from the ground. Built into the fuselage is a retractable step that pulls down. One foot into the stirrup...

...and the next foot onto the wing.

The Hurricane pilot, after all the preparation and effort to get him in place to fight the oncoming enemy, is alone in his fighter.

Below: No. 85 Squadron, commanded by Squadron Leader Peter Townsend, became operational in the night-fighter role in November 1940.

Next page: Michael Turner's painting illustrates the Hurricanes of No. 85 Squadron during the Battle of France.

Michael Turner

Left: The BBMF Hurricane IIC over the countryside of Lincolnshire.

Bottom right: An early photo-reconnaissance Hurricane flown to Calcutta in 1942. The camera fairing is just visible aft of the wing trailing edge. White rings were added to the roundels to avoid confusion with the Japanese red disc.

Left: Sidney Camm's crowning creation, the Hawker Hurricane, silhouetted against the sun.

Below: A Hurricane IIB takes off at dusk for a night patrol.

ACKNOWLEDGMENTS

This book would not have been possible without the enormous contributions of the following people and organizations. Ron and I would like to thank them for their valuable help and assistance.

Tony Ditheridge, Hawker Restorations Ltd.,
Moat Farm, Milden, Suffolk UK
This remarkable organization has researched and brought back to life the unique engineering that made the Hurricane the legendary fighter it was. Their attention to the smallest detail makes their restorations stand alone among other Hurricanes. The crew who returned the subject of this book to a living, breathing airplane are Adrian Gooderham, Nick Baulf, Paul Merser, Richard Watson, Phil Parrish, Bob Young, Mark Schofield, Hugh Smith, Graham Self, Jenny Batley and Deputy Chief Engineer Craig Charleston.

Clive and Linda Denney, Vintage Fabrics, Earls Colne, Essex, UK
The Denneys, an inseparable married team, have thoroughly researched the time-tested methods of assembling fabric-covered aircraft. Through their unique talents and their dedication to their craft, they ensure the preservation of those techniques that evolved during aviation's early years. Clive also painted the Hurricane featured in this book and recreated Douglas Bader's nose art. They and their sons Andrew and Glenn make any visit to East Anglia an enjoyable experience.

Squadron Leader Paul Day, Battle of Britain Memorial Flight, RAF Coningsby
The "Major" and his Flight preserve and fly some of the great RAF aircraft of World War II. Paul Day has always opened the doors and made us feel welcome.

Guy Black, Aero Vintage, for his help with the complex spar manufacture and design.

Bob Cunningham, Steve Vizard, Airframe Assemblies.

Michael Turner
One of the world's premier aviation artists. His paintings make it possible to "see" an event that has been recorded only in memories, creating a wonderful experience – the enjoyment of a piece of fine art *and* a sense of being there.

Glenn Denney
A "Living Historian" who became a fighter pilot for this book.

Cheryl Patterson
Best friend and understanding wife and partner.

Paul Dick
Always tolerant and understanding of a writer's foibles.

Nate, Brigitta and Joe Patterson
They've grown up with these projects and accept the fact that "Dad" is a little crazy chasing old airplanes around.

Tom Patterson
Big thanks to the Quark guru.

Paddy and Tina Worth
Our dear friends who have supported us for many years through their friendship and the wonderful B&B near Thaxted, Essex

Donald Nijboer
Another compatriot and author with whom we've shared a few experiences – there's more to come.

Francis K. Mason
The black-and-white photographs illustrating the text are from Frank's unique collection. His help in finding just the right images and his generosity in allowing their reproduction are greatly appreciated.

Dennis David
Our friend for many years, Dennis is the epitome of the Hurricane pilot. A veteran of both the Battle of France and the Battle of Britain, his insights into flying the Hurricane in combat have been invaluable.

Steve Silburn
Steve provided most of the rare and wonderful artifacts from the RAF and the early stages of the war. In addition to finding and preserving these rare items, he also recreates them.

John Denison, Boston Mills Press
John has believed in and supported what we are doing, as have his colleagues, Kathy Fraser, Noel Hudson and Bill Hanna.

BIBLIOGRAPHY

Armitage, Michael. *The Royal Air Force: An Illustrated History*. London: Arms and Armour Press, 1993

March, Daniel J, ed. *The Aerospace Encyclopedia of Air Warfare*. London: Aerospace Publishing, 1997

Jablonski, Edward. *Air War*. New York: Doubleday, 1979

Mason, Francis K. *The British Fighter since 1912*. London: Putnam, 1992

Green, William and Gordon Swanborough. *The Complete Book of Fighters*. New York: Smithmark, 1994

Bowyer, Chaz. *Hurricane at War*. London: Ian Allan, 1974

Jacobs, Peter. *Hawker Hurricane*. Marlborough, England: The Crowood Press, 1998

Fozzard, John W., ed. *Sydney Camm and the Hurricane*, Washington: Smithsonian Institution Press, 1991

Mason, Francis K. *Battle Over Britain*. London: McWhirter Twins Ltd, 1969

Wood, Derek and Derek Dempster. *The Narrow Margin*. London: Tri-Service Press, 1990

Mason, Francis K. *Aces of the Air*. New York: Mayflower Books, 1981

Shores, Christopher. *Air Aces*. Greenwich, Connecticut: Bison Books, 1983

Bowyer, Chaz. *For Valour: The Air VCs*. London: William Kimber, 1978

Townsend, Peter. *Duel of Eagles*. New York: Simon & Schuster, 1970

David, Dennis. *Dennis "Hurricane" David*. London: Grub Street, 2000

Dan Patterson is a self-employed photographer, graphic designer, and private pilot living in Dayton, Ohio. His previous books include
Shoo Shoo Baby: A Lucky Lady of the Sky
The Lady: Boeing B-17 Flying Fortress
The Soldier: Consolidated B-24 Liberator
Mustang: North American P-51
Lancaster: RAF Heavy Bomber
Messerschmitt Bf 109: Luftwaffe Fighter
Spitfire: RAF Fighter
Thunderbolt: Republic P-47
American Eagles: A History of the United States Air Force
*Cockpit: An Illustrated History of World War II
      Aircraft Interiors.*

Ron Dick served for thirty-eight years in the Royal Air Force, accumulating over 5,000 hours in more than sixty types of aircraft. He retired from the service as an Air Vice-Marshal in 1988 following a tour as the British Defence Attache in Washington, D.C. He now lives in Virginia, writing and lecturing generally on military and aviation history. His previous books include
Lancaster: RAF Heavy Bomber
Messerschmitt Bf109: Luftwaffe Fighter
American Eagles: A History of the United States Air Force

Photo by Cheryl Behner Patterson